I.T.'s Guide to Making SOx a Non-Event

A Concise, Common Sense Approach

by
Stephen J. Casper

Dedicated to my lovely bride, Rachel.

All that is good in my life flows from you.

Contents

INTRODUCTION

The Sarbanes-Oxley Act (SOx) has been with us since July 2002. Since then many of us have done research, leveraged our professional experience and tapped professional contacts in hopes of finding ways to simplify compliance. If you are reading this, you are likely asking, "How do I minimize the cost and distraction of SOx?"

My research and networking led me to vendors and consultants trying to sell something, or to documentation written for auditors (painfully long documentation, I might add). It quickly became evident that there was a lack of clear, concise materials for Information Technology (IT) professionals. This brief guide was written to fill that gap.

So what has been the barrier to simplifying SOx? My conclusion is that ineffective communication between auditors and IT professionals has been the primary problem. This communication gap parallels the challenges IT has faced in working with our business users for many years. The difference is, thus far, we have remained in a reactive posture and allowed auditors to drive the SOx conversation.

IT Management needs to take the lead and drive SOx control and testing work from a risk perspective. Based on a clear understanding of the SOx risks, IT Management needs to ensure the scope is properly set, and then confidently perform testing and move on with life.

The approach proposed in this guide draws on my own experiences in leadership and hands-on roles in technology, audit and control, and quality management. So you ask, "Can SOx become a non-event?" My answer is YES!

This guide creates a cornerstone for a shared understanding of SOx for the entire IT organization. Chapters 8 through 10 provide detailed guidance to SOx practitioners on how to simplify SOx using proven IT methods.

IT's Guide to Making SOx A Non-Event provides practical advice on how to minimize the operational impact of SOx, drive down the cost of SOx controls, reduce SOx audit fees, and increase value from the SOx process. The ideas in this guide do not require expensive software, complex new thinking or consulting fees.

Chapter 1

What SOx Is About

SOx Legislation Overview

Simply stated, SOx is about investor confidence. As we each make our investment decisions in the market either directly or through our 401(k), we assume that the information upon which we are basing our decisions is accurate. Without high levels of confidence and trust, Wall Street and other markets would suffer as well as your 401(k) and mine. We need look no further than the daily newspaper to see evidence of this.

We have all heard about the corporate accounting scandals where senior executives, sometimes with the collusion of their auditors, misled investors and the market with tragic results. So in 2002 the Sarbanes-Oxley Act was born, or SOx as it is more commonly known. The legislation got its name from the two sponsors of the legislation: Senator Paul Sarbanes of Maryland, and Representative Michael Oxley of Ohio.

There are those who say the SOx legislation would not have uncovered the scandals that drove its creation. Maybe yes, and maybe no, but that is water under the bridge because SOx is here for the foreseeable future.

The SOx legislation has many sections, but the two main sections of SOx that impact Information Technology (IT) are:

1. <u>Section 404: Assessment of Internal Control</u>
   This section requires that Management identify and document controls that support accurate financial processing, and then test these controls at least annually to ensure that they are operating properly. Under 404, Management must assert that controls are operating effectively as of December 31 each year.

2. <u>Section 302: Internal Control Certifications</u>
   This section requires that corporate executives (usually the CEO and CFO) personally certify the accuracy of the financial statements submitted for public consumption. Corporate executives largely base their certification on the results of the 404 work. There are both quarterly and annual 302 certifications.

The SOx Process
So SOx is about understanding the risks related to preparing accurate financial statements and the controls Management has in place to mitigate those risks. Management goes through a series of steps (described in Chapter 2) to set the SOx scope, perform testing and fix any problems identified. External auditors perform their own assessment in order to give an opinion on the accuracy of the financial statements.

Ultimately, the SOx process culminates in the CEO and CFO certifying, with the supporting opinion from the external audit firm, the accuracy of the financial statements.

Types of Deficiencies

As Management performs its Section 404 assessments or testing of controls, Management will find problems or deficiencies. Levels of deficiencies depend on the size of the possible impact on the financial statements: *Material weakness* is the highest level, followed by *significant deficiency*, and least serious, a *control deficiency*. The higher the deficiency level, the greater the risk of a financial statement error that would impact investor decisions.

Material weaknesses must be reported to investors (e.g., Wall Street), whereas significant deficiencies are usually only reported internally to the Board of Directors and the Audit Committee. Control deficiencies are shared with Management at a detail level and reported to executives on an aggregated basis.

To be clear, what sends executives to jail is lack of transparency on the company's actual financial situation, not poor management of the company. Executives need to accurately account for their decisions, good or bad, so the investors can make informed choices.

Public Company Accounting Oversight Board

The SOx legislation also created the Public Company Accounting Oversight Board (PCAOB), which is essentially the watchdog over the auditors. The PCAOB establishes standards that the auditors must follow as they perform their external SOx audit activities. In 2007, the PCAOB issued clearer, simpler guidance to auditors (AS5 standard), which replaced the older, more daunting guidance (AS2 standard).

AS5 opened the door to important changes that give Management the ability to reduce the costs and operational impacts of SOx, including:

• SOx work should focus on the areas of greatest risk, e.g. where a material misstatement of the financials is reasonably possible or probable. Remember, SOx is not an internal audit focused on finding all of the deficiencies.

• Auditors may rely more heavily on Management's internal testing based on risk of the control, and objectivity and competence of the tester. The lowest level of reliance is given for high-risk controls where the Control Owners perform their own testing.

• Auditors can consider the results of previous-year audits when planning the nature and extent of the current year's SOx work. Prior to AS5, each year had to stand on its own so auditors could not leverage the success of previous years.

AS5, blended with the repetitive nature of SOx, provides the opportunity to integrate SOx work into normal IT operations and make SOx a non-event.

Key SOx Players
The most common players in a SOx program include:

• SOx Project Management Office (SOx PMO) – Defines and drives the SOx program on behalf of corporate executives. In some organizations, Internal Audit plays the SOx PMO role.

- <u>Process Owners</u> – Own processes containing SOx controls and usually certify internally on the proper operation of their controls, based on testing.

- <u>Control Owners and/or Operators</u> – Own and operate the SOx controls within a process.

- <u>SOx Testers</u> – Perform the tests to ensure that controls are operating properly. SOx Testers can be either Control Operators or independent testers.

- <u>External Auditors</u> – Perform independent assessment of SOx controls and provide their opinion in the company's annual financial statements.

Chapter 2

WHAT DETERMINES THE IT SCOPE

It Starts with the Business Side

I am often asked what brought an application or an infrastructure component into scope. The tone and expression of the person asking typically resembles someone who is talking to his doctor about a "condition"... something incurable in this case!

Setting the SOx scope begins with the financial team performing an analysis of the financial statements. The financial team focuses on financial statement line items with large balances, large transaction volumes or those where Management has a high degree of judgment in setting the value. Since SOx is focused on the accuracy of financial statements, the bigger the number, the higher the chance it could have a material impact on the accuracy of the financial statements if it were wrong.

The accounting concept of materiality drives the selection of financial statement line items and their supporting general ledger accounts (accounts). Materiality is the dollar value that would be considered large enough for an investor or the market to care about. Materiality is often set at 5% of the company's pre-tax profits. So a company with $50 million in profits before tax would have a materiality level of $2.5 million.

Some of the accounts that jump to mind are not necessarily the highest risk accounts. For example, even though payroll has a large dollar and transaction volume, there is a built-in control that generally ensures the accounting is correct... and that is you and the IRS! Both of you notice if you don't get your money.

Actually, the highest-risk accounts are those where there is significant judgment in setting the value. These are called critical accounting estimates. For example, loan loss reserves (how much a company sets aside to cover loans that will not be collectable) are based on complex mathematical modeling that drives the calculation of the loss reserve balances. Even a small percentage of error can result in a material difference in profitability of a company. The rapid changes in the mortgage industry demonstrate all too well the risks and complexity associated with setting loan loss reserves.

Once the accounts have been selected, Management identifies the scope of business processes that are critical to the accuracy of these accounts. For example, the accuracy of loan origination accounts may rely on multiple business processes beginning with loan commitment through the ultimate closing on the loan.

Key Business-Side Controls
Selected business processes are evaluated to identify key financial processing risks and the controls implemented to mitigate those risks. Key controls identified in business processes are either manual, hybrid or application controls.

- <u>Manual Controls</u> are just that… manual. For example, a manager reviews loan papers and signs off that the underwriting work has been completed.

- <u>Hybrid Controls</u> are a mix of manual and application functionality. For example, a manager reviews and corrects rejected transactions using an automated report. For the control to work properly, both the manual and automated parts need to function correctly. If the report is incorrect, the manager cannot completely review rejected transactions.

- <u>Application Controls</u> are based purely on application functionality. For example, an application might perform critical edits that ensure accuracy of processing.

Identifying IT's Scope

It's likely you already get the connection. What brings applications into scope is that the SOx business processes are relying upon application functionality that are labeled as hybrid or application controls. In the above hybrid example, the report brought the application into scope. In the application control example, the edit functionality brought the application into scope.

Once the application is in scope, it may pull with it the underlying infrastructure components including database, operating system, etc., and their related processes for change management and the like.

Understanding exactly what hybrid or application controls brought an application into scope is important for two reasons:

1. Making sure the proper rigor was applied in determining if an application and supporting infrastructure needs to be brought into scope, and

2. Understanding the critical SOx functionality an application contains in order to provide effective governance.

Monitoring which applications are brought into scope is important, as the financial team may be conservative. It is not uncommon for them to bring into scope any application a business process uses, which leads to a bloated SOx application list and wasted money. Reconciliation controls are a common area for scoping mistakes. For example, a control that reconciles two applications using system-generated reports will actually identify errors in the reports. So the applications don't need to be in scope for SOx because the control uses the reports, but doesn't rely on them for the control to work properly.

Understanding the SOx application and hybrid controls that brought an application into scope provides specificity that is useful in governing a SOx application. For example, as an owner of a SOx application, your testing practices will receive more scrutiny. Knowing what application functionality delivers hybrid and application controls allows you to proactively manage testing to ensure changes don't unintentionally impact them.

When the SOx application scope has been set, the infrastructure components that support the applications may be brought into scope as well. Determining whether the supporting infrastructure comes into scope requires a clear understanding of the risk that the infrastructure presents to the specific hybrid or application controls.

Unfortunately, it is not uncommon for the SOx business and IT functions to work independently. It is important that you take a strong stance on the integration of the two or you will most assuredly have a bloated SOx IT scope and less effective program.

Chapter 3

IT GENERAL CONTROLS... THE FOCUS OF IT

Understanding IT General Controls

With the SOx application and infrastructure scope identified, the focus shifts to IT General Controls (ITGCs). ITGCs provide reasonable assurance that IT processes will protect the application functionality (hybrid and application controls) and the data that the business relies upon for accurate financial processing.

ITGCs are embedded in application and infrastructure support processes such as change management, incident management, access provisioning, etc. For example, ITGCs embedded in the change management process ensure that new and changed programs are properly authorized and tested before they are placed into production.

ITGCs are broken into operational controls and monitoring controls. Operational controls are embedded in the normal day-to-day IT processes, while monitoring controls more often focus on periodic reviews. For example, an *operational control* for provisioning user access to applications would be requiring the approval of the application owner. A common *monitoring control* for user provisioning would be a quarterly review of user access to ensure that provisioning controls are working correctly. A strong monitoring control would include root-cause analysis and correction of identified provisioning problems.

Although a company will have many controls, Management needs to decide which key controls they rely upon for SOx. Only key SOx controls are tested for Section 404 compliance. Monitoring controls are often selected as key controls.

Categories of ITGCs

Although there are variances between companies and their external auditors, the scope of SOx ITGCs usually includes:

- <u>Application Development</u> – Ensures that new applications and application changes are developed in a controlled fashion with appropriate user involvement.

- <u>Change Management</u> – Ensures changes are properly tested and approved before they are placed into production. Change management practices consider appropriate segregation of duties between users, developers, change management staff and operations staff.

- <u>Access Management</u> – Ensures that access to production programs and data is aligned with the change management and business segregation of duties models. SOX focuses on the ability of application users, and privileged system and database administrators to update production programs and data.

- <u>Operations Management</u> – Ensures that normal operations are executed properly, incidents are addressed in a timely fashion, and operational backups exist to restore processing as needed. Disaster recovery planning is excluded for SOx.

- <u>Security Management</u> – Ensures that infrastructure components are appropriately hardened so that access management controls cannot be bypassed.

Use of centralized processes, scheduling tools, backup tools, development methodologies, and the like make your job easier. This guide does not elaborate on specific ITGCs as most firms have established them at this point.

Chapter 4

HOW CONTROLS GET EVALUATED

Testing Overview

Compliance with SOx 404 requirements is accomplished through a blend of Management and external auditor testing. In certain cases, the SOx PMO may perform some testing as well. The SOx PMO and the external auditors should work closely with Management to ensure there is no overlap.

Although many companies test more frequently, Management and external auditors are only required to test controls annually.

Management's Testing

Management testing approaches vary from company to company but generally fall into two categories: (1) Management self-assessment and (2) independent testing. Management's approach to testing greatly influences how external auditors approach their SOx work.

Management self-assessment (MSA), as it implies, has Control Owners perform testing of their own SOx controls. Independent testing occurs when Management engages qualified staff other than Control Owners to perform testing of Management's key controls and report their findings. Independent testers can be either an internal dedicated function or an external firm.

Advocates of MSA generally believe that having Control Owners perform the testing of their control increases their knowledge and ownership. Further, there is a belief that MSA is less expensive as internal staff, rather than specialized internal staff or expensive external consultants, are performing the work.

However, my view is that independent testing provides the highest quality outcome. SOx Control Owners are rarely qualified auditors, objective enough to perform testing, or passionate about doing audit-like work (hard to believe, I know). To be clear, SOx Control Owners still own the controls and are accountable for their effective operation when using independent testing. SOx Control Owners can be as effective in their role when they are the customers of independent testing rather than performing the testing themselves.

On the cost front, independent testing delivers a lower-cost or cost-neutral result as it:

• <u>Reduces audit fees</u> - external auditors can place more reliance on independent testing than on MSA, and independent testing rates should be lower than external auditor rates.

• <u>Lowers operational impact</u> - independent testing gets done faster as the staff is highly trained.

• <u>Eliminates MSA handholding</u> - the time needed to support Control Owners during MSA is costly and generally overlooked.

So independent testing provides higher assurance of quality at a lower or neutral cost. If I were the person at risk of going to jail, the choice would be easy.

External Audit Testing
Once Management completes testing, the external auditors will complete their work during the third and early fourth quarter of a company's fiscal year. A key component of the auditor's plan is the amount of reliance they can place on Management's testing as follows:

• Reliance on Management's testing – When auditors can place full or partial reliance on Management's testing. This is most often the case with low risk control areas such as backups, batch scheduling, etc.

• Reuse of Management's evidence – When auditors cannot rely on Management's testing, they can often reuse the evidence management used. For example, auditors can reuse the same system-generated evidence used to perform Management testing.

• No reliance – When auditors cannot rely on Management's testing or evidence, they will request their own evidence, usually because of the importance of the control. For example, auditors must request their own sample for change management testing even when they place partial reliance on Management's testing.

The higher the reliance and reuse, the lower your audit fees and impact on your staff.

Exceptions vs. Deficiencies

It is useful to distinguish between a testing exception and SOx deficiency. The former is when a SOx tester finds any variation while conducting testing. The latter occurs in a classification process involving the Process Owner, Control Owner and the SOx PMO. Ultimately the SOx PMO has the final say on which testing exceptions become deficiencies.

Exceptions become deficiencies unless the exception is determined to be an anomaly. For example, if your initial test found that 1 of 20 items had an error, but a follow-up test of another 20 items found no errors, then you could make the case the 1 error was an anomaly. It is important to note that you can't argue a key control isn't important once you find a problem.

Sometimes while researching an exception, it is determined that another control mitigates or compensates for the risk of the control exception. For example, testing identifies that several terminated employees' application access was not identified for removal during a quarterly access review. Subsequent research determines that network access was removed, which compensates for the risk related to application access. Although this will be a deficiency, Management should evaluate if the network access control is actually the key SOx control for terminations.

Standard Testing Terms

Some standard audit terms you will want to know are:

- Operational Control – An action that provides reasonable assurance that the objectives of a process will be attained.

- Monitoring Control – A practice that assesses the performance of operational controls, and fixes the root cause of problems identified.

- Testing – The practice of validating that controls are operating as designed.

- Exception – Any variation found in testing.

- Exception Classification – The process of evaluating testing exceptions to determine if they will become deficiencies, and if so, what level of deficiency.

- Design Deficiency – When a control is poorly designed and, as a result, does not provide reasonable assurance that a process's objectives will be attained.

- Operating Deficiency – When a control is not operating as it was designed.

- Compensating Control – When a control compensates for the failure of another control. To be relied upon for SOx purposes, the compensating control needs to have been tested.

- Population – The total number of items a control processed in the time period under review.

- Sample – The subset of items you must evaluate or test in order to be reasonably assured that the control is working properly. The SOx PMO will have standard sample sizes based on the frequency the control operates.

- Expected Error Rate – The percentage of testing exceptions found in the sample. For example, if you select a sample of 20 changes from a population of 1,000 changes and determine that 5 of the 20 changes have exceptions, you have an expected error rate of 25% (5/20 = 25%). So the total projected errors in the population are 250 or 25% of 1,000.

- Walk-through – When Management brings an auditor up-to-speed on how a process and its controls work. Typically an auditor will look for an example or a "test of one" when participating in a walk-through to better understand the process.

- Segregation of Duties (SOD) – Separating duties between functions to ensure that no individual role can bypass controls. For example, application developers are responsible for developing applications, while the change management staff is responsible for deploying changes to production. The segregation of duties helps ensure that the change management process and its controls cannot be bypassed.

Chapter 5

WHAT SOX IS NOT ABOUT

The Right Focus

You need to be relentless on this point - SOx is about reasonable (not absolute) assurance—that material financial errors will be caught and corrected in a reasonable period of time.

The PCAOB goes further to state "it is not necessary to test controls that, even if deficient, would not present a reasonable possibility of material misstatement to the financial statements."

Business processes can and do have problems, and SOx controls are designed to catch those problems. As long as controls identify problems in a reasonable period of time, they are not SOx deficiencies. From a practical standpoint, a reasonable period of time is before the financial statements are released for public consumption.

For example, let's say as you write checks all month long you have a bad habit of not logging checks into your register, resulting in overdrafts to your account. That being said, you faithfully enter your checks and balance your checking account at the end of each month. From a SOx perspective, you are fine as you have properly accounted for your unfortunate overdraft charges and the checkbook is accurate in a reasonable period of time.

It is important to note that during non-SOx audits, Internal Audit will have a different stance on your approach to checkbook management, as they are concerned with appropriate use of funds as well.

Good Enough

Another perspective that often gets lost is that SOx is not best practice-oriented. If an Information Security Policy states that applications should have eight-character, alphanumeric passwords, but a SOx application only has a seven-character password; you don't have a SOx deficiency. There is no credible position that your actual practice results in a "reasonable possibility" of a material financial statement error. It is good enough! It is a different story if you have a two-character password.

That being said, Management should be keenly interested in setting and following relevant policies and standards that ensure they have a well-controlled computing environment. But these types of variances are not deficiencies from the SOx perspective.

Chapter 6

SOX – WHY HAS IT BEEN A BIG DEAL?

The Big Secret
SOx is about blocking and tackling concepts that IT professionals learn early in their careers, such as testing programs, or making sure the user approves changes before they are put into production.

So what has the big deal been about? A number of factors have contributed to the SOx confusion, including the original legislation's lack of specificity and the angst with which it was accepted. The three primary gaps that persist are communication, view of deficiencies and evidencing requirements.

Communication
We have long discussed and/or lamented the communication gap that exists between business and IT professionals. In response, we have created specialized roles such as business analysts and developed many techniques to help bridge this gap. Most importantly, we see the gap!

We have a similar, or perhaps greater, gap that exists between Audit and IT professionals. Controls have not traditionally been a key component of IT professionals' formal education or on-the-job training, or at least not labeled as such. As we noted above, user involvement and testing are examples of IT basics, but we don't label them as controls per se. And although IT auditors have familiarity with IT processes and controls, they typically have not had much practitioner experience.

This communication gap is made worse by IT's historical relationship with auditors, underpinned by "gotcha-oriented" auditors and "don't ask, don't tell" IT engagement. Typically auditors would show up every two or three years and ask a bunch of questions. Auditors would find a number of deficiencies, propose solutions that IT found impractical, and disagreement would ensue. Eventually IT Management would relent and fix the deficiencies whether they made sense or not.

The auditors' professional requirement to remain objective and independent only widens the gap. Auditors can provide feedback on ideas, but they can't directly participate in defining control improvements, as they would no longer be objective on subsequent audits. That is why auditors can't tell you what to do.

View of Deficiencies
It has been my experience that SOx deficiencies and audit findings are often viewed as an indicator that Management doesn't know what it is doing. For example, it is not uncommon to see goals like "we don't want any deficiencies." SOx is about reasonable assurance; it is unlikely that there is a credible cost-benefit proposition that supports zero deficiencies.

The focus needs to be on finding and fixing deficiencies, and managing the trend down over time. The incremental reduction in new deficiencies and eliminating repeat deficiencies represents performance, not the absolute number of deficiencies.

Each year the SOx program will get smarter, dig deeper and find new deficiencies... that is a good thing!

The key challenge to finding and fixing deficiencies is really on the motivational side... why would your staff want to do it? As long as deficiencies are viewed negatively with an adverse impact on performance ratings and bonuses, the continuous improvement (find and fix) process will be hobbled. A negative view of deficiencies reinforces hiding and secretly fixing problems, the exact opposite behavior SOx tries to foster.

The quality movement evolved along a similar path until finding and fixing defects became a positive. IT's goal is to have a well-controlled, high-performing function with or without SOx. If you want to strengthen a control environment quickly, recognize and reward employees for deficiencies found and fixed!

Evidencing Requirements

Any audit activity, including SOx, is about providing evidence that the controls needed to mitigate key risks are working properly. This is commonly a point of contention for SOx and audits alike. In many cases, IT processes and their controls are not designed to archive evidence and auditors cannot simply take our word for it.

Clearly identifying the evidence needed to demonstrate that SOx controls are working properly, and then delivering it, is likely the most time-consuming part of the SOx work. In the early stages of a SOx program it can seem like you are on a scavenger hunt for SOx evidence.

Unlike the traditional 3-year audit cycle, SOx evidence needs to be produced each year. The repetitive nature of SOx drives the value proposition that control procedures and SOx evidence management fulfill, as discussed in later chapters.

Chapter 7

REPOSITIONING SOX

Resetting the Paradigm

Thus far, auditors have driven the SOx conversation. IT Management needs to take the lead and drive a proactive SOx control environment, one that manages SOx risks within the context of adding value to the business.

SOx controls, and ITGCs in general, are intended to reduce the likelihood of bad things happening. Think in terms of cars having dummy lights, brakes, and many features that didn't directly influence your decision to buy a car. You simply expect them to be there, or you would likely have a serious problem with your purchase.

A well-designed SOx program aligns with Management's interest to drive continuous improvement in the timeliness, accuracy and completeness of IT operations. This requires a clear, pragmatic set of SOx controls that are embedded into normal operations.

Key Principles

To reposition SOx, we must start with a few basic principles:

- Controls are a normal part of our processes and evidence is a natural by-product;

- IT Management owns IT general controls (ITGCs) in support of the business;

- ITGCs deliver reasonable assurance that IT processes are working properly; and

- ITGCs provide the foundation for effective business process controls.

Along with these principles, the measures of success need to be improved in order to recognize and reward finding and fixing problems and ensuring they don't recur. The ability to make mistakes, talk openly about problems and collaborate on solutions is the mark of a high-performing company.

Chapter 8

SIMPLIFYING SOX

The Solution

The repetitive nature of SOx lends itself to being operationalized. Simplifying SOx requires a clear understanding of the controls and the evidence that demonstrates the control is operating effectively. Developing detailed control procedures and deploying evidence management processes will provide the solution.

The following provides an introduction to control procedures and evidence management processes. Each is described in more detail in subsequent chapters.

Control Procedures

Control procedures are the cornerstone to making SOx a non-event as they define specifically what is performed. This is like any other desktop procedure. It is essential that you engage the SOx PMO in designing and documenting control procedures. The key is to make sure the control procedure and the evidence it generates are aligned with internal and external audit requirements.

SOx Evidence Management

Evidence management provides the framework to gain agreement on, and efficiently store and deliver evidence. Key components of evidence management include:

- <u>Evidence Dictionary</u> – Describes each piece of evidence and its quality assurance procedure, and provides an evidence example and standard request form (if needed).

- <u>Evidence Schedule</u> – Details the timing for (1) receipt of evidence used to operate controls if evidence is requested from a third party, and (2) control execution and filing of the evidence of control operation.

- <u>Evidence Vault</u> – An optional central storage location for evidence that can be a simple, secured directory or a more sophisticated document management solution.

- <u>Evidence Management and Metrics</u> – Provide operational and retrospective reporting on normal operations and any gaps identified.

Depending on your company's specific approach to SOx, you can expect the operational evidence management activities to require one full-time equivalent (FTE). Staffing may be impacted if you decide to manage testing evidence using the evidence management process.

Chapter 9

CONTROL PROCEDURES

It's That Simple

Control procedures provide a detailed description of the control and the evidence it generates. Most organizations have documented SOx processes and control descriptions unless the company or specific controls have only recently become subject to SOx. Generally SOx control descriptions are high-level and do not provide the specificity needed to operationalized the SOx work.

An example of a control description might be "programmers are not allowed update access to the production environment." Relying on control descriptions leads to a vicious cycle of explaining controls and discovering the appropriate evidence with what can sometimes seem like a never-ending stream of auditors.

Control procedures identify the inputs the control uses, control process steps, and the output the control generates. This approach applies basic process modeling techniques that have existed for more than 20 years with a few control/audit twists added.

SOx control procedures should minimally include the following:

Control Component	Description
Scope	The applications or infrastructure covered by the control.
What	The specific procedural steps performed.
Who	The position or group that performs the control. For example, the Production Turnover Team. Do not use specific peoples names.
Frequency	The number of times the control operates in a certain time period.
Evidence	What inputs were used to perform the control and what outputs were created from operating the control.
Population (Monitoring controls only)	The total number of items the control processed during the time period under review.
Sample (Monitoring controls only)	The number of items you selected to review and how you picked them based on the frequency the control operates.
Policy and Standard (optional)	Consider including the policy and standard that a control procedure implements, although you need to be careful that you are not held to the best practice-level for SOx.

Important Note: Once control procedures are defined and agreed between Control Owners and the SOx PMO, it is vital that the controls be followed. If not, you will receive a deficiency when the auditors perform their review. Following the procedure "most of the time" is not good enough.

Evidence Labeling

Within the control procedure, evidence should be described at a logical level such as "system-generated directory access listing." The physical description will be documented in the Evidence Dictionary. To ensure clear linkage of evidence defined in the control procedure and the Evidence Dictionary, Evidence Identification Numbers (EINs) should be assigned.

An example of an EIN format would be CC-CN-EI where:

• Control Category (CC) – Such as "UA" for user access, "CM" for change management, etc.

- Control Number (CN) – A sequential number for each control in the category.

- Evidence Identifier (EI) – A sequential number assigned to identify each type of evidence for a control. Alternatively, you may want to consider using a label such as "Prelist."

As referenced in the Appendix, Example 2, the EIN for the system-generated list of users used as input to the UA-01 control is EIN: UA-01-02, where:

- UA is the user access control category;

- 01 is the control number assigned for the periodic review of privileged access; and

- 02 is the evidence identifier for the system-generated prelist.

Note: A sub-type label would be added to the EIN to identify different types of physical evidence that exist for UA-01-02 such as Oracle, MSSQL, etc.

Other Considerations and Opportunities
Reducing Cost of Controls
Controls procedures provide a basis to estimate the cost of control and target high-cost controls for improvement. Optionally, time tracking can be used to collect actual time spent to validate estimates. Management may be startled at how much time is being spent on SOx controls.

In some cases, the frequency of controls can be reduced based on the track record of findings. For example, if the results of a monitoring control over a period of time demonstrate that the operational control is working effectively, a case can be made for reducing the frequency of the monitoring control.

Change and Configuration Management

It is vital that changes to controls and evidence management components are managed through a formal process. As with the formal change management process for application program changes, control and evidence management component changes need to be vetted by appropriate groups and deployed on a coordinated basis.

Since controls are under change and configuration management, auditors can easily assess what has changed since their last testing cycle. Stable controls allow auditors to reduce their testing and related fees.

Chapter 10

EVIDENCE MANAGEMENT

Evidence Dictionary

The most important component when deploying evidence management is the Dictionary. The Dictionary defines key evidence attributes needed to support complete and accurate fulfillment and storage of evidence. Again, it is essential that you engage the SOx PMO, as the evidence defined must be auditable.

Dictionary Basics

Each type of evidence noted in the control procedures has at least one Dictionary entry. Each Dictionary entry should have a description, quality assurance requirements, example, and standard request form if evidence is received from a third party.

System-generated evidence is the strongest evidence as it cannot be easily altered. For example, if you were performing the access review described in the Appendix, Example 2, the output spreadsheet of users without the supporting system-generated list of users would not provide sufficient evidence, because you might have simply created the spreadsheet without having performed the underlying work.

In certain situations the logical evidence referenced in a control procedure may relate to several different applications or technologies. In these cases, the logical evidence may have different types of physical evidence. For example, the database-generated evidence for reviewing privileged DBA access varies between database technologies. Separate Evidence Dictionary sub-type entries are used in this situation.

<u>Dictionary Entries</u>
The dictionary entries should include the following:

• Evidence Identification Number (EIN) – Assigned in the control procedure.

• Sub-Type – Used when different physical types of evidence exist for an EIN.

• Evidence Name – Name or label given to the evidence.

• Purpose – What the evidence is demonstrating.

• Type – Input (used to perform the control) or Output (evidence of control operation).

• Frequency and Schedule – How often and in what months the evidence is produced in an annual SOx cycle. The actual date is not included here as it is established when creating the Evidence Schedule.

• Evidence Owner – The role or group that owns and is responsible for the evidence. Typically the Evidence Owner is the Control Owner.

• Evidence Storage Location – This is particularly important if an Evidence Vault is not used.

• Complexity (optional) – Amount of time required to produce the evidence.

In cases where evidence management is additionally used to facilitate receipt of input evidence from third parties such as an internal data center or vendor, entries should include:

• Requestor(s) – Who is requesting this evidence.

• Fulfiller – The role or group who will provide the evidence.

Quality Assurance Requirements
The quality assurance requirements define the specific attributes used to assess the correctness of the evidence. The quality assurance requirements are typically reasonableness characteristics such as size of file, date generated, etc. The Control Owner is responsible for maintaining (or submitting to the Vault if used) the correct evidence.

Evidence Example
An example of the evidence is an extremely important tool to ensure you get the correct evidence. It is even more important for insulating you against staff turnover of control operators, evidence suppliers and auditors. A picture really is worth a thousand words!

Standard Request Form
If fulfillment of input evidence from third parties is managed through the Evidence Schedule, it is useful to have a predefined request form to expedite the receipt of evidence. It is important that both the requestor and the fulfiller agree upon the standard request form for a specific piece of evidence.

Other Considerations and Opportunities

Having the evidence documented in the Dictionary provides an opportunity to evaluate and simplify evidence. As you initially document evidence, you will likely uncover a fair amount of inconsistency in what gets delivered. Standardization may enable you to reduce cost and improve the consistency of control operation.

Documenting the complexity (i.e., time required) to create each type of evidence can be useful for identifying high-cost evidence, as it is not always readily apparent. Complexity information is useful in identifying areas where there may be a value proposition for the use of automation.

Evidence Schedule

The Evidence Schedule (Schedule) provides a detailed calendar of when evidence will be available throughout a year. Information in the Dictionary is the driver for preparing the Schedule. An annual Schedule that is revised quarterly is a good starting point.

The Schedule should minimally include the following. The descriptions below assume that evidence is being delivered to the Vault.

- Evidence Identifier Number (EIN) – Assigned in the control procedure.

- Sub-Type – Used when different physical types of evidence exist for an EIN.

- Evidence Name – Name or label given to the evidence.

- Type – Input (used to perform the control) or Output (evidence of control operation).

- Evidence Owner – The role or group that owns and is responsible for the evidence.

- Original Due Date – The initially agreed-to delivery date.

- Revised Due/Delivery Date – The revised due date or actual date the evidence was received. Enter the actual date of receipt in the revised due date field when received.

- Status – Blank, Late or Filled.

- On-time Flag – Yes or No. Set when the evidence is filled.

- Comments – This section provides pertinent notes and is used for the narrative of conversations when evidence is late.

In cases where evidence management is additionally used to facilitate receipt of input evidence from third parties (such as an internal data center or vendor), entries should include:

- Requestor – The group who is requesting the evidence.

- Fulfiller – The group who will provide the evidence.

The Schedule is an important tool for managing workflow and auditor expectations. It enables simple pipeline reporting and metrics. You will quickly find that auditors are extremely interested in looking at the schedule so they can develop their own schedules.

A spreadsheet is the easiest starting point for a scheduling tool. Spreadsheet pivot tables are useful for preparing tracking reports and metrics.

Example Schedule

The following is an example Schedule for evidence related to the periodic review of access described in the Appendix, Example 2. There are three applications (A, B, and C) in scope.

EIN/Sub-Type	Evidence Name	Type	Requestor	Fulfiller	Original Due Date	Revised Due Date/ Delivery	Status	On-Time Flag	Comments
				Example Evidence Schedule as of 05/17					
UA-01-01-App A	SOD Model	Input	Access Team	Business Team	05/15	05/15	Filled	Yes	
UA-01-01-App B	SOD Model	Input	Access Team	Business Team	05/15	05/15	Filled	Yes	
UA-01-01-App C	SOD Model	Input	Access Team	Business Team	05/15	05/15	Filled	Yes	
UA-01-02-App A	Directory relist	Input	Access Team	Vendor #1	05/15	05/13	Filled	Yes	
UA-01-02-App B	Directory Prelist	Input	Access Team	Vendor #1	05/15	05/30	Late		5/13 – vendor indicated it would be delivered on 5/30
UA-01-02-App C	Directory Prelist	Input	Access Team	Vendor #1	05/15	05/30	Late		5/13 – vendor indicated it would be delivered on 5/30
UA-01-03-App A	Review Spreadsheet	Output	--	Access Team	06/15				
UA-01-03-App B	Review Spreadsheet	Output	--	Access Team	06/15				
UA-01-03-App C	Review Spreadsheet	Output	--	Access Team	06/15				

Other Considerations and Opportunities

• Auditor Requests: If you use the Vault, auditors will be able to self-service evidence of Management's control operation. If you don't use the Vault, you will want to schedule auditor's requests to facilitate a smooth SOx audit cycle and to keep the auditors within their budget.

Whether or not the Vault is used, auditors will need to request their own input evidence in certain cases. In these cases, auditors are not always in a position to select their samples when you are preparing the schedule, but you can still have a placeholder request to ensure that the group who will fulfill the request knows it is coming.

- Ad hoc Requests: Situations will arise where ad hoc (i.e., unscheduled) requests are necessary. For example, when auditors find a problem with a control they will likely need to request additional, unplanned information to complete their analysis of the problem. Ad hoc requests should require the use of a standardized form. It is useful to review ad hoc requests to determine if they should be added to the scheduled evidence management process.

Evidence Vault

If you choose to make use of an Evidence Vault (Vault), you can make it as complex or simple as desired. Starting simple and then becoming more sophisticated if necessary is the best choice. Becoming too elaborate too quickly may add unnecessary complexity.

Vault Contents

The Vault contains both the input that controls use, and the output controls create. Based on other systems used, the Vault can optionally store evidence of Management's testing as well.

In some cases it may not make sense to store control input in the Vault. For example, change management monitoring controls often look at a large number of change management tickets and their supporting testing and approval evidence. In these cases, the storage location should be noted in the Evidence Dictionary and auditors should be given direct read access to the storage location if possible.

The Vault can also include other relevant documentation such as process documentation and other items. View the Vault like a grocery store; you want to keep the shelves stocked with items that people want.

Vault Organization
You will most likely want to organize the Vault using a blend of the Evidence Identification Number (EIN) and the SOX period such as 20xx-EIN-Qx. Auditors will usually look at a control's operation and evidence for the full year. Organizing evidence of control operation (and testing if it is stored in the vault) by quarter it is performed is a good starting point.

The naming conventions used in the Vault can be helpful when it comes to assuring that evidence has been filed correctly. For example, if the folder structure parallels the EIN format, you can manually scan a list to identify misfiled evidence, or write a script to identify them.

Vault Access
Control Owners and Operators should not be given update access to their evidence just as developers should not be given update access to their production programs. Control Owners, Control Operators, auditors, etc., should be given inquiry access. It can be useful to establish a centralized mailbox for receipt of evidence and related questions.

Other Considerations and Opportunities
The operational receipt and filing of defined evidence in the Vault can be an inexpensive way to reassure Management that a control is operating. Late, missing or unexpected evidence is an indication that a control is not

operating or has changed outside of the normal change management process. This can be particularly useful for monitoring controls that have had a stable track record.

Evidence Management and Metrics
<u>Roles and Responsibilities</u>

A straw man for evidence management roles and responsibilities is presented in the RASIC chart below. Additional roles beyond those noted in Chapter 1 - *Key SOx Players* include:

• Evidence Analyst is the owner of the Vault and custodian of its contents.

• Evidence Librarian performs the operations and reporting surrounding the Vault.

Activity	Process Owner	Control Owner	Control Operator	Evidence Analyst	Evidence Librarian	SOx PMO/Auditors	3rd Party Fulfillers	Evidence Generated
Manage Control Procedures								
• Develop and maintain Control Procedures	A	R	S	S	S	C*		Control Procedures
• Coordinate evidence management infrastructure updates needed to ensure continued alignment	C		C	A/R	S	C	C	Updates for Vault, Dictionary, and Schedule
Manage the Vault								
• Perform intake including QA, escalate problems and update the Schedule			C	C	A	R		Filed Evidence and Updated Schedule
• Escalate problems with evidence requests								
– Input evidence for control operation			C	C	C		A/R	Email Notification with 24 hours
– Evidence for auditors			A/R	C	C	C		
• Escalate problems with delivered evidence								
– Input evidence for control operation			A/R	C	C		C	Email Notification with 24 hours
– Evidence for auditors			C	C	C	A/R		Email Notification with 24 hours
• Perform cycle audits		S	S	A/R	S		S	Metrics and Correct Evidence
Manage the Dictionary								
• Maintain Dictionary in alignment with Control Procedures			S	A/R	S	C	S	Updated Dictionary Entries
• Prepare or revise standard evidence requests		A	R	S			S	Updated Standard Requests
Manage the Schedule								
• Establish SOx Program schedule and key dates	I	I	I	I	I	A/R		
• Prepare annual Schedule and conduct quarterly updates		S	S	A/R	S	S		Updated Schedule
• Prepare scheduled and ad hoc SOx audit requests				S		A/R		Scheduled SOx Audit Requests
• Fulfill scheduled and ad hoc requests		A	R	S	S	S		Evidence
Manage Performance								
• Communicate performance and metrics	I	I	I	A/R	S	I		Metrics and Status Reports
• Manage delays and problems	C	S	S	A/R	S	I		Escalation Emails and Updates
• Perform gap tracking and drive continuous improvement		S	S	A/R	S	S	S	Gap Reporting and Improvement Recommendations

Roles and Responsibilities (Responsible, Accountable, Support, Inform, and Consult)

* SOx PMO approval is required

Status Reporting and Metrics

Tracking and reporting of control operation status and gaps is essential to generating confidence with IT Management and auditors alike. You want to ensure individual fulfillers are accountable and visible for their performance, as well as measure gaps within the context of the overall volume of items processed. For example, 50 gaps may sound like a large number, but if 4,000 items were filed, it is only a 1.25% error rate.

A sample of reports and metrics you may want to consider include:

• Evidence pipeline management metrics:

- Number of scheduled items submitted to the vault vs. the total for the quarter (% complete)

- Number of late items by fulfiller (used for escalation)

- Rolling 30-Day Schedule (simplified report for keeping a short-term focus)

• Process improvement metrics:

- On-time delivery percentage in total, and by fulfiller for input evidence and Evidence Owner for output evidence.

- Percentage of items returned for quality reasons in total, and by fulfiller.

- Number of missing items identified by testing and/or auditors in total, and by Evidence Owner.

Conclusion

The goal of this guide is to change the way you look at SOx. In everything else we do as IT professionals, we are methodical about understanding requirements and cost-effectively addressing them. Thus far, we have not consistently applied that tried-and-true paradigm in addressing SOx requirements.

IT Management needs to drive pragmatic SOx control and testing work based on a clear understanding of the SOx risks. Although Auditors can be an excellent resource, IT needs to take the lead in establishing a high-performing, well-controlled IT computing environment.

It is difficult to take the lead without a well-defined approach. Ad hoc approaches lead to a never-ending cycle of educating an array of auditors, conducting evidence scavenger hunts, and struggling to educate the next set of Control Operators. It is like a never-ending nightmare!

Well-written SOx control procedures and strong SOx evidence management provide the answer for minimizing the operational and financial impact of SOx, including:

- Reducing operational impact as Control Owners clearly understand their controls and what evidence auditors need, and are storing it as a normal part of control operation. No more evidence scavenger hunts!

- <u>Reducing audit fees</u> as the evidence that auditors need is clearly understood and documented in advance and readily available through self-service if an Evidence Vault is used. No more training the new wave of auditors!

- <u>Managing the cost of controls</u> as clearly-defined controls can have budgeted and actual time-related costs tracked. Imagine having the data you need to understand and reduce the cost of SOx controls!

- <u>Reducing the impact of staff turnover</u> as clearly-defined controls and supporting evidence management processes simplify knowledge transfer. Sweet resilience!

Enjoy your journey to making SOx a non-event!

Appendix – Control Procedure Examples

Both of these example control procedures target the risk of unauthorized access to applications and support a high-level control of "privileged user access to applications should be appropriate based on job duties."

1. User Access Provisioning Control (Operational Control)

• <u>Scope</u>: Application A, Application B and Application C.

• <u>What</u>: Requests for privileged access to in-scope applications are evaluated to ensure that the appropriate application owner approval exists on the Access Request Form.

• <u>Who</u>: Application System Administrator.

• <u>Frequency</u>: As needed.

• <u>Evidence</u>:

  – Inputs: Approved Access Request Forms (EIN)

  – Outputs: Reviewed Access Request Forms (EIN)

2. Periodic Review of Application User Access (Monitoring Control)

• <u>Scope</u>: Application A, Application B and Application C.

• <u>Population</u>: All privileged application users.

- <u>Sample</u>: Not applicable - all users with privileged access are reviewed.

- <u>What</u>: Review a system-generated list of privileged application users and verify that their access is appropriate based on the segregation of duties model (SOD).

- <u>Who</u>: Business Application Owner or Delegate.

- <u>Frequency</u>: Quarterly.

- <u>Evidence</u>:

  - Inputs: SOD model (EIN: UA-01-01) and systems-generated list of users with privileged access to the in-scope applications (EIN: UA-01-02)

  - Outputs: Spreadsheet of privileged users, their job title, a yes/no indication of the appropriateness of access, and the action taken to remove inappropriate access (EIN: UA-01-03)